A SPIRITUAL GUIDE FOR
PERMANENT WEIGHT LOSS

LOSE IT *for* LIFE

Interactive JOURNAL PLANNER

STEPHEN ARTERBURN, M. ED.

JANELLE PUFF

MISTY CONAWAY

INTEGRITY®
PUBLISHERS
Nashville

INTRODUCTION

To be a true "Loser For Life" does not mean just losing weight, but losing our resistance to God's best for our lives. We can begin to care for God's good creation in every part of us—spiritual, emotional, mental, and physical.

This journal planner is designed to help you take care of your whole self. We hope it will be a useful tool in planning and recording meals and exercise during your first 60 days in the Lose It For Life program. Although it's intended for daily use, if you miss a day—or several—don't give up! Just jump in where you left off, with no shame or condemnation.

In order to help you get started, refer to the sample page that follows to see what a day's food and exercise plan might entail. The eight water glass icons each represent eight ounces of fluid, for a daily total of 64 ounces. Use them as a reminder, and shade them in throughout the day so that you may chart and reach your water intake goal.

For times when you are tempted to take that first compulsive bite, which may well trigger a binge, we have provided an appendix called "Before I Nibble in Excess . . ." We encourage you to make a contract with yourself involving the probing questions on this page. Rather than an unrealistic vow never to overeat again, promise yourself that before you indulge, you will first read and respond to these questions. They have been provided as a buffer between craving and consumption. Dedicate yourself to at least five minutes of honest reflection here and see what happens with your eating.

Also, a second appendix is provided for when you have strayed from your plan. It is easy in these times to slip into guilt and shame over our failures and spiral into hopelessness. Instead of allowing yourself to get too far down that path, follow the action steps for getting back on the recovery track. Then return to the day's plan, right where you are.

We trust that the space and questions provided for journaling throughout this book will encourage you to consider God's direction in staying on track for your complete and lasting recovery. It is meant to be helpful, inspirational, and convenient.

In your personal journey with God toward weightlessness and healthfulness in all areas of your life, remember you are loved and never alone. Be open and honest, and willing to reflect and learn about yourself. Listen to God. And reach for humility.

God is with you, and so are we!

The Authors

SAMPLE

_ord, with You, I care for my **body** today . . .

Here is my food plan:

B 2 eggs, 1 cup yogurt, 1 cup blueberries,
   coffee

S 1 oz low sugar cereal with half banana &
   4 oz milk

L 3 oz chicken, 2 cups salad, 2 tbsp dressing,
   apple

S 1 tbsp almond butter with celery

D 3 oz turkey/beef combo burger, 1 cup
   broccoli, 1 cup salad, 1 medium sweet potato
   with butter substitute

I remembered my water!

Alterations:
_Rushed through breakfast; salad not available at
lunch, substituted with veggie soup; busy with
kids, so ate dinner late + frozen yogurt_

My plan for activity and rest:
_30 min. speed-walk outside, 50 crunches, 5 min.
weight lifting (arms); stairs instead of elevators
at work; in bed by 11pm/sleep at least 7 hours_

Alterations:
Nope, I did it!!! Felt so good to accomplish.

DAY 1

Lord, with You, I care for my **spirit** today . . .

Whoever finds his life will lose it, and whoever loses his life for my sake will find it. — *MATTHEW 10:39*

What do I hope to "gain" by losing weight?

_____

_____

_____

_____

Lord, with You, I care for my **emotions** today . . .

Emotions Check-In:

_____

_____

_____

_____

Lord, with You, I care for my **mind** today . . .

I will train myself to know this is not deprivation; I am choosing life.

What did I do well today (name at least one thing)?

_____

What am I grateful for today?

_____

What will I need God to help me with tomorrow?

_____

_____

Lord, with You, I care for my **body** today . . .

Here is my food plan:

B *(Breakfast)*

S *(Snack)*

L *(Lunch)*

S *(Snack)*

D *(Dinner)*

I remembered my water!

[8 OZ] [8 OZ] [8 OZ] [8 OZ] [8 OZ] [8 OZ] [8 OZ] [8 OZ]

Alterations:

My plan for activity and rest:

Alterations:

Additional thoughts, notes, insight, goals, dreams . . .

DAY 2

Lord, with You, I care for my **spirit** today . . .

"Oh, there is so much more I want to tell you, but you can't bear it now. When the Spirit of truth comes, he will guide you into all truth . . . " —JOHN 16:12-13 NLT

Am I willing to let God set the pace for my healing?

Lord, with You, I care for my **emotions** today . . .

Emotions Check-In:

Lord, with You, I care for my **mind** today . . .

In seeking for answers regarding my weight loss, I know God will reveal all that I need for today.

What did I do well today (name at least one thing)?

What am I grateful for today?

What will I need God to help me with tomorrow?

Lord, with You, I care for my **body** today . . .

Here is my food plan:

B

S

L

S

D

I remembered my water!
Alterations:

My plan for activity and rest:

Alterations:

HELPFUL TIP:

When eating a meal, eat it slowly. Allow your body the chance to recognize that it is filling up before the entire plate is consumed.

Additional thoughts, notes, insight, goals, dreams . . .

DAY 3

Lord, with You, I care for my **spirit** today . . .

You shall do no wrong in judgment, in measurement of weight, or capacity. You shall have just balances, just weights . . . I am the LORD your God, who brought you out from the land of Egypt. —LEVITICUS 19:35-36 NASB

How have I allowed the scale to dictate how I feel about myself?

Lord, with You, I care for my **emotions** today . . .

Emotions Check-In:

Lord, with You, I care for my **mind** today . . .

I will remember to use the scale for measuring my weight, not my worth.

What did I do well today (name at least one thing)?

What am I grateful for today?

What will I need God to help me with tomorrow?

Lord, with You, I care for my **body** today . . .

Here is my food plan:

B

S

L

S

D

I remembered my water!
Alterations:

8 OZ	8 OZ	8 OZ	8 OZ	8 OZ	8 OZ	8 OZ	8 OZ

My plan for activity and rest:

Alterations:

Additional thoughts, notes, insight, goals, dreams . . .

DAY 4

Lord, with You, I care for my **spirit** today . . .

Therefore do not worry about tomorrow, for tomorrow will worry about itself. Each day has enough trouble of its own. — MATTHEW 6:34

Have I been so daunted by the long-term nature of recovery that I have immobilized myself from doing what I can do today?

Lord, with You, I care for my **emotions** today . . .

Emotions Check-In:

Lord, with You, I care for my **mind** today . . .

I will focus on what I need to do today, and tomorrow's recovery will care for itself.

What did I do well today (name at least one thing)?

What am I grateful for today?

What will I need God to help me with tomorrow?

Lord, with You, I care for my **body** today . . .

Here is my food plan:

B

S

L

S

D

I remembered my water!
Alterations:

| 8 OZ | 8 OZ | 8 OZ | 8 OZ | 8 OZ | 8 OZ | 8 OZ | 8 OZ |

My plan for activity and rest:

Alterations:

Additional thoughts, notes, insight, goals, dreams . . .

DAY 5

Lord, with You, I care for my **spirit** today . . .

*Ask and it will be given to you; seek and you will find;
knock and the door will be opened to you. For everyone
who asks receives; he who seeks finds; and to him who
knocks, the door will be opened.* —MATTHEW 7:7-8

How has the daily routine of asking, seeking, and
knocking opened the door to lifelong recovery from
food and weight problems for me?

Lord, with You, I care for my **emotions** today . . .

Emotions Check-In:

Lord, with You, I care for my **mind** today . . .

*I will consider the benefits of continually going to God
for help.*

What did I do well today (name at least one thing)?

What am I grateful for today?

What will I need God to help me with tomorrow?

Lord, with You, I care for my **body** today . . .

Here is my food plan:

B

S

L

S

D

I remembered my water!

Alterations:

My plan for activity and rest:

Alterations:

Additional thoughts, notes, insight, goals, dreams . . .

DAY 6

Lord, with You, I care for my **spirit** today . . .

One who was there had been an invalid for thirty-eight years. When Jesus saw him lying there and learned that he had been in this condition for a long time, he asked him, "Do you want to get well?" —JOHN 5:5-6

How have I sabotaged progress with my food and weight problems, thereby crippling my efforts to be healthy?

_____

_____

_____

Lord, with You, I care for my **emotions** today . . .

Emotions Check-In:

_____

_____

Lord, with You, I care for my **mind** today . . .

Instead of lying here for another 38 years, I will lay down my excuses and take action today.

What did I do well today (name at least one thing)?

_____

_____

What am I grateful for today?

_____

_____

What will I need God to help me with tomorrow?

_____

_____

Lord, with You, I care for my **body** today . . .

Here is my food plan:

B

S

L

S

D

I remembered my water! [8 OZ] [8 OZ] [8 OZ] [8 OZ] [8 OZ] [8 OZ] [8 OZ] [8 OZ]

Alterations:

My plan for activity and rest:

Alterations:

HELPFUL TIP:

Get a great pair of supportive running/walking/cross-training shoes. Give your body the legitimate, helpful supplies you need for meeting your exercise goals. Having the right equipment at the right time can make the difference between resignation and perseverance. Just be careful not to get tricked into gadgets!

Additional thoughts, notes, insight, goals, dreams . . .

DAY 7

Lord, with You, I care for my **spirit** today . . .

Can a man scoop fire into his lap without his clothes being burned? Can a man walk on hot coals without his feet being scorched? — PROVERBS 6:27-28

How can I improve the safety of my eating environment today?

Lord, with You, I care for my **emotions** today . . .

Emotions Check-In:

Lord, with You, I care for my **mind** today . . .

I will consider the many resources God has provided to help me live the healthy life.

What did I do well today (name at least one thing)?

What am I grateful for today?

What will I need God to help me with tomorrow?

Lord, with You, I care for my **body** today . . .

Here is my food plan:

B

S

L

S

D

I remembered my water! [8 OZ] [8 OZ] [8 OZ] [8 OZ] [8 OZ] [8 OZ] [8 OZ] [8 OZ]
Alterations:

My plan for activity and rest:

Alterations:

HELPFUL TIP:

When shopping at the grocery store, avoid your own personal trigger foods as much as possible, or limit the amount you purchase to one-serving packages. If you dare to buy ice cream, steer clear of the large tubs. Only purchase the smallest version available—and try the low-fat, no sugar added. If you want to have pretzels, buy the low-sodium, one-serving-bag size that goes with one lunch. Protect your home environment from bingeing supplies!

Additional thoughts, notes, insight, goals, dreams . . .

DAY 8

Lord, with You, I care for my **spirit** today . . .

> *"There's a young boy here with five barley loaves and two fish. But what good is that with this huge crowd?" . . . the men alone numbered five thousand . . . Jesus took the loaves, gave thanks to God, and passed them out to the people. Afterward he did the same with the fish. . . . And they all ate until they were full. —J O H N   6 : 9 - 1 1   N L T*

In what ways have I dismissed a smaller portion size as insignificant when compared to my immense hunger?

Lord, with You, I care for my **emotions** today . . .

Emotions Check-In:

Lord, with You, I care for my **mind** today . . .

> *I will remember that in releasing my portions, God's power will be unleashed to satisfy my cravings in a way I never expected.*

What did I do well today (name at least one thing)?

What am I grateful for today?

What will I need God to help me with tomorrow?

Lord, with You, I care for my **body** today . . .

Here is my food plan:

B

S

L

S

D

I remembered my water! 🥛 🥛 🥛 🥛 🥛 🥛 🥛 🥛

Alterations:

My plan for activity and rest:

Alterations:

Additional thoughts, notes, insight, goals, dreams . . .

DAY 9

Lord, with You, I care for my **spirit** today . . .

Jesus said to him, "If you wish to be complete, go and sell your possessions and give to the poor, and you will have treasure in heaven; and come, follow Me." But when the young man heard this statement, he went away grieving . . . —MATTHEW 19:21-22 NASB

In what ways have I become so attached to food that I've missed God's true path for me?

Lord, with You, I care for my **emotions** today . . .

Emotions Check-In:

Lord, with You, I care for my **mind** today . . .

Instead of walking away grieving, I will remember that by surrendering my hold on food, all that I lose is the destruction that goes with it.

What did I do well today (name at least one thing)?

What am I grateful for today?

What will I need God to help me with tomorrow?

Lord, with You, I care for my **body** today . . .

Here is my food plan:

B

S

L

S

D

I remembered my water!

Alterations:

My plan for activity and rest:

Alterations:

HELPFUL TIP:

GOOD FOR THE . . .

Brain—carrots, broccoli, fish, fruits and vegetables high in antioxidants

Eyes—Foods rich in Vitamins C, E, and lutein (kale, collard greens, citrus fruits, cantaloupe)

Lungs—Foods high in beta carotene (mangos, carrots, pumpkin, spinach, red peppers)

Heart—fruits, vegetables, grains, fat-free and low-fat foods, fish, lean meats, legumes

Bones—dairy products, dark green leafy vegetables, almonds, sesame or sunflower seeds

Skin—foods rich in beta carotene

Colon—high-fiber foods (oats, fruits, vegetables)

Additional thoughts, notes, insight, goals, dreams . . .

DAY 10

Lord, with You, I care for my **spirit** today . . .

The younger son told his father, "I want my share of your estate now, instead of waiting until you die." So his father agreed to divide his wealth between his sons.
—*LUKE 15:12 NLT (from the story of the Prodigal Son)*

Have I compulsively and prematurely demanded a larger portion of food instead of waiting for a normal portion at the correct time?

Lord, with You, I care for my **emotions** today . . .

Emotions Check-In:

Lord, with You, I care for my **mind** today . . .

I will humbly acknowledge that I have already had my share of sweet, salty, and rich foods—enough for a lifetime.

What did I do well today (name at least one thing)?

What am I grateful for today?

What will I need God to help me with tomorrow?

Lord, with You, I care for my **body** today . . .

Here is my food plan:

B

S

L

S

D

I remembered my water! [8 OZ] [8 OZ] [8 OZ] [8 OZ] [8 OZ] [8 OZ] [8 OZ] [8 OZ]

Alterations:

My plan for activity and rest:

Alterations:

Additional thoughts, notes, insight, goals, dreams . . .

DAY 11

Lord, with You, I care for my **spirit** today . . .

*When he finally came to his senses, he said to himself,
"At home even the hired men have food enough to spare,
and here I am, dying of hunger!"* —LUKE 15:17 NLT
(from the story of the Prodigal Son)

Do I see the reality of my situation—a place where I
never thought I would find myself?

Lord, with You, I care for my **emotions** today . . .

Emotions Check-In:

Lord, with You, I care for my **mind** today . . .

*I will stop looking at restriction and deprivation in diets,
and accept that a food plan brings freedom.*

What did I do well today (name at least one thing)?

What am I grateful for today?

What will I need God to help me with tomorrow?

Lord, with You, I care for my **body** today . . .

Here is my food plan:

B

S

L

S

D

I remembered my water!   8 oz | 8 oz | 8 oz | 8 oz | 8 oz | 8 oz | 8 oz | 8 oz
Alterations:

My plan for activity and rest:

Alterations:

Additional thoughts, notes, insight, goals, dreams . . .

DAY 12

Lord, with You, I care for my **spirit** today . . .

I will go home to my father and say, "Father, I have sinned against both heaven and you, and I am no longer worthy of being called your son. Please take me on as a hired man." —LUKE 15:18-19 NLT (from the story of the Prodigal Son)

Have I devised my plan of action for recovery today?
Am I ready to work for my success?

Lord, with You, I care for my **emotions** today . . .

Emotions Check-In:

Lord, with You, I care for my **mind** today . . .

I will make my food plan a priority, acknowledging that self-indulgence has led to emptiness and feelings of unworthiness.

What did I do well today (name at least one thing)?

What am I grateful for today?

What will I need God to help me with tomorrow?

Lord, with You, I care for my **body** today . . .

Here is my food plan:

B

S

L

S

D

I remembered my water! | 8 OZ | 8 OZ | 8 OZ | 8 OZ | 8 OZ | 8 OZ | 8 OZ | 8 OZ |

Alterations:

My plan for activity and rest:

Alterations:

Additional thoughts, notes, insight, goals, dreams . . .

DAY 13

Lord, with You, I care for my **spirit** today . . .

> *So he returned home to his father. And while he was still
> a long distance away, his father saw him coming. Filled
> with love and compassion, he ran to his son, embraced
> him, and kissed him. His son said to him, "Father, I have
> sinned against both heaven and you, and I am no longer
> worthy of being called your son." —LUKE 15:20-21 NLT*
> (from the story of the Prodigal Son)

In my past failures regarding food and weight, have I
viewed God as filled with love and compassion for me?

Lord, with You, I care for my **emotions** today . . .

Emotions Check-In:

Lord, with You, I care for my **mind** today . . .

> *Regardless of how many mistakes I've made or how many
> pounds I have yet to lose, no matter how slowly the pounds
> come off, I know I can always return to the Father.*

What did I do well today (name at least one thing)?

What am I grateful for today?

What will I need God to help me with tomorrow?

Lord, with You, I care for my **body** today . . .

Here is my food plan:

B

S

L

S

D

I remembered my water!
Alterations:

[8 OZ] [8 OZ] [8 OZ] [8 OZ] [8 OZ] [8 OZ] [8 OZ] [8 OZ]

My plan for activity and rest:

Alterations:

Additional thoughts, notes, insight, goals, dreams . . .

DAY 14

Lord, with You, I care for my **spirit** today . . .

I prayed to the LORD, and he answered me, freeing me from all my fears. —PSALM 34:4

What fears do I have? Here is my list:

Lord, with You, I care for my **emotions** today . . .

Emotions Check-In:

Lord, with You, I care for my **mind** today . . .

I know that fear is a primary activator of unbridled eating, but I also know that the Lord will deliver me.

What did I do well today (name at least one thing)?

What am I grateful for today?

What will I need God to help me with tomorrow?

Lord, with You, I care for my **body** today . . .

Here is my food plan:

B

S

L

S

D

I remembered my water!   8 OZ 8 OZ 8 OZ 8 OZ 8 OZ 8 OZ 8 OZ 8 OZ
Alterations:

My plan for activity and rest:

Alterations:

Add some mushrooms to your meals! They are fat-free, low in calories, and high in minerals. Mushrooms can enhance nearly every dish you make, and they are reportedly a great immune system booster.

Additional thoughts, notes, insight, goals, dreams . . .

DAY 15

Lord, with You, I care for my **spirit** today . . .

Jumping out of the boat, Peter walked on the water to Jesus. But when he looked down at the waves churning beneath his feet, he lost his nerve and started to sink. He cried, "Master, save me!" Jesus didn't hesitate. He reached down and grabbed his hand. —MATTHEW 14:29-31 MSG

How has food been my "boat," keeping me afloat and dependent on it and yet isolating me from others?

Lord, with You, I care for my **emotions** today . . .

Emotions Check-In:

Lord, with You, I care for my **mind** today . . .

When the waves of life churn and I crave comfort food, I will remember to take a risk and step out of my boat. I know You will take my hand.

What did I do well today (name at least one thing)?

What am I grateful for today?

What will I need God to help me with tomorrow?

Lord, with You, I care for my **body** today . . .

Here is my food plan:

B

S

L

S

D

I remembered my water!
Alterations:

My plan for activity and rest:

Alterations:

Additional thoughts, notes, insight, goals, dreams . . .

DAY 16

Lord, with You, I care for my **spirit** today . . .

I have come that they may have life, and that they may have it more abundantly. — JOHN 10:10 NKJV

How can I focus on diminishing deprivation and living an abundant life today?

Lord, with You, I care for my **emotions** today . . .

Emotions Check-In:

Lord, with You, I care for my **mind** today . . .

I will remember that focusing on deprivation will magnify deprivation. But life becomes abundant when I focus on God's provision.

What did I do well today (name at least one thing)?

What am I grateful for today?

What will I need God to help me with tomorrow?

Lord, with You, I care for my **body** today . . .

Here is my food plan:

B

S

L

S

D

I remembered my water! 8 OZ 8 OZ 8 OZ 8 OZ 8 OZ 8 OZ 8 OZ 8 OZ

Alterations:

My plan for activity and rest:

Alterations:

Additional thoughts, notes, insight, goals, dreams . . .

DAY 17

Lord, with You, I care for my **spirit** today . . .

. . . I keep working toward that day when I will finally be all that Christ Jesus saved me for and wants me to be. . . . I am focusing all my energies on this one thing: Forgetting the past and looking forward to what lies ahead . . .
—*PHILIPPIANS 3:12-13 NLT*

Looking back as early as five minutes ago, what is one destructive behavior about food that I need to leave behind me?

Lord, with You, I care for my **emotions** today . . .

Emotions Check-In:

Lord, with You, I care for my **mind** today . . .

I will focus my thoughts on the hope of what lies ahead; of the reason Jesus saved me, even into the next five minutes.

What did I do well today (name at least one thing)?

What am I grateful for today?

What will I need God to help me with tomorrow?

Lord, with You, I care for my **body** today . . .

Here is my food plan:

B

S

L

S

D

I remembered my water!

☐ 8 OZ ☐ 8 OZ ☐ 8 OZ ☐ 8 OZ ☐ 8 OZ ☐ 8 OZ ☐ 8 OZ ☐ 8 OZ

Alterations:

My plan for activity and rest:

Alterations:

HELPFUL TIP:

Instead of pouring on dressing or even dipping your food into the condiments, simply dip your fork first; then load the bite. Even the smallest adjustments will have the greatest impact over time . . . in either direction.

Additional thoughts, notes, insight, goals, dreams . . .

DAY 18

Lord, with You, I care for my **spirit** today . . .

But the Lord answered and said to her, "Martha, Martha, you are worried and bothered about so many things . . . "
—LUKE 10:41 NASB

How does frantic activity affect my overeating?

Lord, with You, I care for my **emotions** today . . .

Emotions Check-In:

Lord, with You, I care for my **mind** today . . .

I will guard against mindless consumption by hearing the voice of Jesus calling me to let go of worry.

What did I do well today (name at least one thing)?

What am I grateful for today?

What will I need God to help me with tomorrow?

Lord, with You, I care for my **body** today . . .

Here is my food plan:

B

S

L

S

D

I remembered my water!   [8 OZ] [8 OZ] [8 OZ] [8 OZ] [8 OZ] [8 OZ] [8 OZ] [8 OZ]
Alterations:

My plan for activity and rest:

Alterations:

Additional thoughts, notes, insight, goals, dreams . . .

DAY 19

Lord, with You, I care for my **spirit** today . . .

> *And a woman who had been suffering from a hemorrhage for twelve years, came up behind Him and touched the fringe of His cloak; for she was saying to herself, "If I only touch His garment, I will get well." But Jesus turning and seeing her said, "Daughter, take courage; your faith has made you well." —MATTHEW 9:20-22 NASB (emphasis added)*

Do I believe I deserve recovery enough to risk becoming visible?

Lord, with You, I care for my **emotions** today . . .

Emotions Check-In:

Lord, with You, I care for my **mind** today . . .

> *In daring faith, I will consistently take the risk of reaching for recovery on all levels.*

What did I do well today (name at least one thing)?

What am I grateful for today?

What will I need God to help me with tomorrow?

Lord, with You, I care for my **body** today . . .

Here is my food plan:

B

S

L

S

D

I remembered my water!

Alterations:

My plan for activity and rest:

Alterations:

Additional thoughts, notes, insight, goals, dreams . . .

DAY 20

Lord, with You, I care for my **spirit** today . . .

For I envied the proud when I saw them prosper despite their wickedness. They seem to live such a painless life; their bodies are so healthy and strong. They aren't troubled like other people or plagued with problems like everyone else. —PSALM 73:3-5 NLT

Have I felt a sense of unfairness that others can seemingly eat what they want without gaining a pound?

Lord, with You, I care for my **emotions** today . . .

Emotions Check-In:

Lord, with You, I care for my **mind** today . . .

I will not compare my inner challenges about food and weight with the appearance of others.

What did I do well today (name at least one thing)?

What am I grateful for today?

What will I need God to help me with tomorrow?

Lord, with You, I care for my **body** today . . .

Here is my food plan:

B

S

L

S

D

I remembered my water! [8 OZ] [8 OZ] [8 OZ] [8 OZ] [8 OZ] [8 OZ] [8 OZ] [8 OZ]

Alterations:

My plan for activity and rest:

Alterations:

Additional thoughts, notes, insight, goals, dreams . . .

DAY 21

Lord, with You, I care for my **spirit** today . . .

Don't store up treasures here on earth, where they can be eaten by moths and get rusty, and where thieves break in and steal. Store your treasures in heaven, where they will never become moth-eaten or rusty and where they will be safe from thieves. Wherever your treasure is, there your heart and thoughts will also be. —MATTHEW 6:19-21 NLT

How have I treasured food over God in my life?

Lord, with You, I care for my **emotions** today . . .

Emotions Check-In:

Lord, with You, I care for my **mind** today . . .

I will nurture the thought that living by my plan for health is actually a plan for enjoying life on earth while storing up treasures in heaven.

What did I do well today (name at least one thing)?

What am I grateful for today?

What will I need God to help me with tomorrow?

Lord, with You, I care for my **body** today . . .

Here is my food plan:

B

S

L

S

D

I remembered my water! 🥛 🥛 🥛 🥛 🥛 🥛 🥛 🥛
Alterations:

My plan for activity and rest:

Alterations:

HELPFUL TIP:

The lack of water, just like the lack of food, will slow your metabolism. Water is the body's most important nutrient. Without it, the liver will focus on water retention rather than on burning fat.

Additional thoughts, notes, insight, goals, dreams . . .

DAY 22

Lord, with You, I care for my **spirit** today . . .

Now my soul is deeply troubled. Should I pray, "Father, save me from what lies ahead"? But that is the very reason why I came! Father, bring glory to your name.
—*JOHN 12:27-28 NLT*

Am I prepared to accept that the death of my will may involve times of excruciating pain?

Lord, with You, I care for my **emotions** today . . .

Emotions Check-In:

Lord, with You, I care for my **mind** today . . .

Though I may dread some of the tasks at hand, I will stay centered on God's purposes in me.

What did I do well today (name at least one thing)?

What am I grateful for today?

What will I need God to help me with tomorrow?

Lord, with You, I care for my **body** today . . .

Here is my food plan:

B

S

L

S

D

I remembered my water!   [8 oz] [8 oz] [8 oz] [8 oz] [8 oz] [8 oz] [8 oz] [8 oz]

Alterations:

My plan for activity and rest:

Alterations:

Enjoy the feeling of cleansing that comes from a good sweat while you exercise.

Additional thoughts, notes, insight, goals, dreams . . .

DAY 23

Lord, with You, I care for my **spirit** today . . .

When I kept silent, my bones wasted away through my groaning all day long. —PSALM 32:3

How will I step out of silence and connect with a fellow "Loser" today?

Lord, with You, I care for my **emotions** today . . .

Emotions Check-In:

Lord, with You, I care for my **mind** today . . .

I will consider how connection keeps me from emotional misery.

What did I do well today (name at least one thing)?

What am I grateful for today?

What will I need God to help me with tomorrow?

Lord, with You, I care for my **body** today . . .

Here is my food plan:

B

S

L

S

D

I remembered my water!
Alterations:

| 8 oz | 8 oz | 8 oz | 8 oz | 8 oz | 8 oz | 8 oz | 8 oz |

My plan for activity and rest:

Alterations:

Additional thoughts, notes, insight, goals, dreams . . .

DAY 24

Lord, with You, I care for my **spirit** today . . .

Remember my affliction and my wandering, the wormwood and bitterness. Surely my soul remembers and is bowed down within me. —LAMENTATIONS 3:19-20 NASB

What experiences of affliction and wandering cause resentment and bitterness within me?

Lord, with You, I care for my **emotions** today . . .

Emotions Check-In:

Lord, with You, I care for my **mind** today . . .

I will consider that although it is painful, looking at my past helps bring resolution.

What did I do well today (name at least one thing)?

What am I grateful for today?

What will I need God to help me with tomorrow?

Lord, with You, I care for my **body** today . . .

Here is my food plan:

B

S

L

S

D

I remembered my water! 🥤🥤🥤🥤🥤🥤🥤🥤

Alterations:

My plan for activity and rest:

Alterations:

Additional thoughts, notes, insight, goals, dreams . . .

DAY 25

Lord, with You, I care for my **spirit** today . . .

Love . . . keeps no record of when it has been wronged.
—1 CORINTHIANS 13:5B NLT

Toward whom have I harbored resentments? What record am I keeping?

Lord, with You, I care for my **emotions** today . . .

Emotions Check-In:

Lord, with You, I care for my **mind** today . . .

Instead of allowing my resentments to trigger destructive eating, I will remember that love frees me.

What did I do well today (name at least one thing)?

What am I grateful for today?

What will I need God to help me with tomorrow?

Lord, with You, I care for my **body** today . . .

Here is my food plan:

B

S

L

S

D

I remembered my water! 🥛 🥛 🥛 🥛 🥛 🥛 🥛 🥛
Alterations:

My plan for activity and rest:

Alterations:

Additional thoughts, notes, insight, goals, dreams . . .

DAY 26

Lord, with You, I care for my **spirit** today . . .

> *But he said to them, "I have food to eat that you know nothing about." Then his disciples said to each other, "Could someone have brought him food?" "My food," said Jesus, "is to do the will of him who sent me and to finish his work." —JOHN 4:32-34*

In my hungriest moments, am I willing to turn to God and allow Him to feed, nourish, and sustain me?

_____

_____

_____

Lord, with You, I care for my **emotions** today . . .

Emotions Check-In:

_____

_____

Lord, with You, I care for my **mind** today . . .

> *I will focus on being nourished by the doing of God's will, especially for my health.*

What did I do well today (name at least one thing)?

_____

What am I grateful for today?

_____

What will I need God to help me with tomorrow?

_____

_____

Lord, with You, I care for my **body** today . . .

Here is my food plan:

B

S

L

S

D

I remembered my water!
Alterations:

| 8 OZ | 8 OZ | 8 OZ | 8 OZ | 8 OZ | 8 OZ | 8 OZ | 8 OZ |

My plan for activity and rest:

Alterations:

Additional thoughts, notes, insight, goals, dreams . . .

DAY 27

Lord, with You, I care for my **spirit** today . . .

> Therefore I tell you, stop being perpetually uneasy
> (anxious and worried) about your life, what you shall
> eat or what you shall drink; *or about your body, what you
> shall put on. Is not life greater [in quality] than food, and
> the body [far above and more excellent] than clothing?*
> —*MATTHEW 6:25 AMP (emphasis added)*

How have I lived in anxious eating, whether obsessing
over food or micromanaging my plan for health?

Lord, with You, I care for my **emotions** today . . .

Emotions Check-In:

Lord, with You, I care for my **mind** today . . .

I will value my spiritual condition more than food.

What did I do well today (name at least one thing)?

What am I grateful for today?

What will I need God to help me with tomorrow?

Lord, with You, I care for my **body** today . . .

Here is my food plan:

B

S

L

S

D

I remembered my water!

Alterations:

My plan for activity and rest:

Alterations:

HELPFUL TIP:

Each time you feel hungry, reach for ice water instead of excess food. Often your body is really trying to tell you it's thirsty.

Additional thoughts, notes, insight, goals, dreams . . .

DAY 28

Lord, with You, I care for my **spirit** today . . .

Therefore I tell you, stop being perpetually uneasy (anxious and worried) about your life, what you shall eat or what you shall drink; or about your body, what you shall put on. Is not life greater [in quality] than food, and the body [far above and more excellent] than clothing?
— MATTHEW 6:25 AMP (emphasis added)

How have I lived in anxiety for my body, obsessing over clothing size or appearance?

Lord, with You, I care for my **emotions** today . . .

Emotions Check-In:

Lord, with You, I care for my **mind** today . . .

I will value the health of my body more than how I dress it up.

What did I do well today (name at least one thing)?

What am I grateful for today?

What will I need God to help me with tomorrow?

Lord, with You, I care for my **body** today . . .

Here is my food plan:

B

S

L

S

D

I remembered my water! 8 oz 8 oz 8 oz 8 oz 8 oz 8 oz 8 oz 8 oz

Alterations:

My plan for activity and rest:

Alterations:

Caffeine stimulates the pancreas to produce insulin. Too much caffeine may lead to unhealthy cravings.

Additional thoughts, notes, insight, goals, dreams . . .

DAY 29

Lord, with You, I care for my **spirit** today . . .

. . . Try me and know my anxious thoughts; and see if there be any hurtful way in me, and lead me in the everlasting way. —PSALM 139:23B-24 NASB

How do I let anxious thoughts hurt my progress toward lasting health and successful weight loss?

Lord, with You, I care for my **emotions** today . . .

Emotions Check-In:

Lord, with You, I care for my **mind** today . . .

I will remember that I need not use food to cope with anxiety.

What did I do well today (name at least one thing)?

What am I grateful for today?

What will I need God to help me with tomorrow?

Lord, with You, I care for my **body** today . . .

Here is my food plan:

B

S

L

S

D

I remembered my water!

Alterations:

My plan for activity and rest:

Alterations:

Additional thoughts, notes, insight, goals, dreams . . .

DAY 30

Lord, with You, I care for my **spirit** today . . .

In his great mercy he has given us new birth into a living hope. . . . In this you greatly rejoice, though now for a little while you may have had to suffer grief in all kinds of trials. —1 PETER 1:3B, 6

How can we allow the joy of our freedom in Christ to help us transcend our trials involving food and weight loss?

Lord, with You, I care for my **emotions** today . . .

Emotions Check-In:

Lord, with You, I care for my **mind** today . . .

In the joy of Christ, I will face the discomfort of new behaviors.

What did I do well today (name at least one thing)?

What am I grateful for today?

What will I need God to help me with tomorrow?

Lord, with You, I care for my **body** today . . .

Here is my food plan:

B

S

L

S

D

I remembered my water! [8 OZ] [8 OZ] [8 OZ] [8 OZ] [8 OZ] [8 OZ] [8 OZ] [8 OZ]

Alterations:

My plan for activity and rest:

Alterations:

HELPFUL TIP:

When you feel like skipping exercise today, insert an Aretha Franklin CD into your "drive!" She'll give you just enough attitude and self-"Respect" to get the job done. Put on songs of upbeat praise that raise your energy and help you focus on the goodness of God. Use music to alter your mood and get your body into high gear!

Additional thoughts, notes, insight, goals, dreams . . .

DAY 31

Lord, with You, I care for my **spirit** today . . .

I know and am perfectly sure on the authority of the Lord Jesus that no food, in and of itself, is wrong to eat. But if someone believes it is wrong, then for that person it is wrong. —ROMANS 14:14 NLT

Am I envious of what others are able to eat, compared to what my body needs?

Lord, with You, I care for my **emotions** today . . .

Emotions Check-In:

Lord, with You, I care for my **mind** today . . .

I will keep my mind on what my body needs, not on what others are eating.

What did I do well today (name at least one thing)?

What am I grateful for today?

What will I need God to help me with tomorrow?

Lord, with You, I care for my **body** today . . .

Here is my food plan:

B

S

L

S

D

I remembered my water!

8 OZ 8 OZ 8 OZ 8 OZ 8 OZ 8 OZ 8 OZ 8 OZ

Alterations:

My plan for activity and rest:

Alterations:

Additional thoughts, notes, insight, goals, dreams . . .

DAY 32

Lord, with You, I care for my **spirit** today . . .

*We remember the fish we ate in Egypt at no cost—
also the cucumbers, melons, leeks, onions and garlic.
But now we have lost our appetite; we never see any-
thing but this manna!* — NUMBERS 11:5 *(The Israelites,
remembering the benefits of their slavery in Egypt)*

Do I engage in self-pity, remembering the benefits of
hot fudge sundaes and forgetting the slavery it caused?

Lord, with You, I care for my **emotions** today . . .

Emotions Check-In:

Lord, with You, I care for my **mind** today . . .

*I will accept the reality that there will be times when I
crave the unhealthy foods which enslaved me. I will
remember that I do not have to act on these cravings.*

What did I do well today (name at least one thing)?

What am I grateful for today?

What will I need God to help me with tomorrow?

Lord, with You, I care for my **body** today . . .

Here is my food plan:

B

S

L

S

D

I remembered my water! [8 oz] [8 oz] [8 oz] [8 oz] [8 oz] [8 oz] [8 oz] [8 oz]

Alterations:

My plan for activity and rest:

Alterations:

Additional thoughts, notes, insight, goals, dreams . . .

DAY 33

Lord, with You, I care for my **spirit** today . . .

No one can serve two masters. Either he will hate the one and love the other, or he will be devoted to the one and despise the other. —MATTHEW 6:24A

How has "serving" food kept me from truly loving and trusting God?

Lord, with You, I care for my **emotions** today . . .

Emotions Check-In:

Lord, with You, I care for my **mind** today . . .

In the moment of decision, I will surrender my love for and grip on food.

What did I do well today (name at least one thing)?

What am I grateful for today?

What will I need God to help me with tomorrow?

Lord, with You, I care for my **body** today . . .

Here is my food plan:

B

S

L

S

D

I remembered my water!   8 OZ 8 OZ 8 OZ 8 OZ 8 OZ 8 OZ 8 OZ 8 OZ

Alterations:

My plan for activity and rest:

Alterations:

HELPFUL TIP:

We need not be shy when asking a restaurant waiter to have our meals prepared to fit our food plan. Most restaurants are eager to accommodate your healthy choices!

Additional thoughts, notes, insight, goals, dreams . . .

DAY 34

Lord, with You, I care for my **spirit** today . . .

For no one can lay any foundation other than the one already laid, which is Jesus Christ. If any man builds on this foundation using gold, silver, costly stones, wood, hay or straw, his work will be shown for what it is . . .
—1 CORINTHIANS 3:11-13A

What messages did I learn from my family that helped to shape my eating behaviors?

Lord, with You, I care for my **emotions** today . . .

Emotions Check-In:

Lord, with You, I care for my **mind** today . . .

In losing it for life, I seek to shape healthy behaviors around eating.

What did I do well today (name at least one thing)?

What am I grateful for today?

What will I need God to help me with tomorrow?

Lord, with You, I care for my **body** today . . .

Here is my food plan:

B

S

L

S

D

I remembered my water! [8 OZ] [8 OZ] [8 OZ] [8 OZ] [8 OZ] [8 OZ] [8 OZ] [8 OZ]

Alterations:

My plan for activity and rest:

Alterations:

HELPFUL TIP:

By engaging in strength training and increasing muscle mass, the body becomes more efficient at burning calories.

Additional thoughts, notes, insight, goals, dreams . . .

DAY 35

Lord, with You, I care for my **spirit** today . . .

Don't become so well-adjusted to your culture that you fit into it without even thinking. Instead, fix your attention on God. —ROMANS 12:2A MSG

In what ways have I fit myself into the culture of "more?"

Lord, with You, I care for my **emotions** today . . .

Emotions Check-In:

Lord, with You, I care for my **mind** today . . .

I will learn to operate on "enough" by fixing my attention on God.

What did I do well today (name at least one thing)?

What am I grateful for today?

What will I need God to help me with tomorrow?

Lord, with You, I care for my **body** today . . .

Here is my food plan:

B

S

L

S

D

I remembered my water!

| 8 OZ | 8 OZ | 8 OZ | 8 OZ | 8 OZ | 8 OZ | 8 OZ | 8 OZ |

Alterations:

My plan for activity and rest:

Alterations:

Additional thoughts, notes, insight, goals, dreams . . .

DAY 36

Lord, with You, I care for my **spirit** today . . .

Charm is deceitful and beauty is fleeting . . .
—*PROVERBS 31:30A*

What messages did I receive as a child that shaped
my body image?

Lord, with You, I care for my **emotions** today . . .

Emotions Check-In:

Lord, with You, I care for my **mind** today . . .

*I will focus my thoughts away from deceptions and into
what You say about my body, Your temple.*

What did I do well today (name at least one thing)?

What am I grateful for today?

What will I need God to help me with tomorrow?

Lord, with You, I care for my **body** today . . .

Here is my food plan:

B

S

L

S

D

I remembered my water!

8 OZ · 8 OZ · 8 OZ · 8 OZ · 8 OZ · 8 OZ · 8 OZ · 8 OZ

Alterations:

My plan for activity and rest:

Alterations:

Additional thoughts, notes, insight, goals, dreams . . .

DAY 37

Lord, with You, I care for my **spirit** today . . .

Search me, O God, and know my heart . . .
—*PSALM 139:23A*

How have I hidden myself from God by engaging in emotional eating?

Lord, with You, I care for my **emotions** today . . .

Emotions Check-In:

Lord, with You, I care for my **mind** today . . .

I will focus on the liberation that comes from being known by God.

What did I do well today (name at least one thing)?

What am I grateful for today?

What will I need God to help me with tomorrow?

Lord, with You, I care for my **body** today . . .

Here is my food plan:

B

S

L

S

D

I remembered my water!

Alterations:

[8 OZ] [8 OZ] [8 OZ] [8 OZ] [8 OZ] [8 OZ] [8 OZ] [8 OZ]

My plan for activity and rest:

Alterations:

HELPFUL TIP:

When you're craving sweets, try a piece of sugarless gum. It will bring pleasure to your mouth, help you burn calories (from the chewing), and will occupy the empty space where food would normally go.

Additional thoughts, notes, insight, goals, dreams . . .

DAY 38

Lord, with You, I care for my **spirit** today . . .

Toward evening they heard the LORD God walking about in the garden, so they hid themselves among the trees. The LORD God called to Adam, "Where are you?"
—GENESIS 3:8-9 NLT

What do I fear will be exposed in me as I release excess food and pounds?

Lord, with You, I care for my **emotions** today . . .

Emotions Check-In:

Lord, with You, I care for my **mind** today . . .

Instead of hiding in shame, I will remember that God calls me into His presence.

What did I do well today (name at least one thing)?

What am I grateful for today?

What will I need God to help me with tomorrow?

Lord, with You, I care for my **body** today . . .

Here is my food plan:

B

S

L

S

D

I remembered my water!

8 OZ | 8 OZ | 8 OZ | 8 OZ | 8 OZ | 8 OZ | 8 OZ | 8 OZ

Alterations:

My plan for activity and rest:

Alterations:

We must realize that one bite or two outside of our healthy eating plan may lead to a binge. We must learn the nutritional value of what we put into our mouths and whether it's going to hurt or help our overall health.

Additional thoughts, notes, insight, goals, dreams . . .

DAY 39

Lord, with You, I care for my **spirit** today . . .

David and all the Israelites were celebrating with all their might before God, with songs and with harps, lyres, tambourines, cymbals and trumpets. — 1 CHRONICLES 13:8

Am I taking time to celebrate my small successes in losing it for life?

Lord, with You, I care for my **emotions** today . . .

Emotions Check-In:

Lord, with You, I care for my **mind** today . . .

I will celebrate what's good in my life and what's great about God.

What did I do well today (name at least one thing)?

What am I grateful for today?

What will I need God to help me with tomorrow?

Lord, with You, I care for my **body** today . . .

Here is my food plan:

B

S

L

S

D

I remembered my water!

[8 oz] [8 oz] [8 oz] [8 oz] [8 oz] [8 oz] [8 oz] [8 oz]

Alterations:

My plan for activity and rest:

Alterations:

Additional thoughts, notes, insight, goals, dreams . . .

_____

_____

_____

_____

_____

_____

_____

_____

_____

_____

_____

_____

_____

_____

_____

_____

_____

_____

_____

_____

DAY 40

Lord, with You, I care for my **spirit** today . . .

> . . . You must not eat fruit from the tree that is in the middle
> of the garden, and you must not touch it, or you will die.
> —GENESIS 3:3

To stay in recovery today, which foods must I not touch?

Lord, with You, I care for my **emotions** today . . .

Emotions Check-In:

Lord, with You, I care for my **mind** today . . .

> I know that not all of my favorite foods are prohibited, but
> I can give up that first bite of what triggers my binges.

What did I do well today (name at least one thing)?

What am I grateful for today?

What will I need God to help me with tomorrow?

Lord, with You, I care for my **body** today . . .

Here is my food plan:

B

S

L

S

D

I remembered my water! [8 oz] [8 oz] [8 oz] [8 oz] [8 oz] [8 oz] [8 oz] [8 oz]

Alterations:

My plan for activity and rest:

Alterations:

Beware of the high carb and caloric content of sodas, fruit juices and alcoholic beverages. It's easy to miss the significant impact in your choice of beverage.

Additional thoughts, notes, insight, goals, dreams . . .

DAY 41

Lord, with You, I care for my **spirit** today . . .

For I am confident of this very thing, that He who began a good work in you will perfect it until the day of Christ Jesus. —PHILIPPIANS 1:6 NASB

What excuses have I used to avoid taking positive steps toward my goal?

Lord, with You, I care for my **emotions** today . . .

Emotions Check-In:

Lord, with You, I care for my **mind** today . . .

As I participate in recovery, I will remain confident that God is perfecting His work in me.

What did I do well today (name at least one thing)?

What am I grateful for today?

What will I need God to help me with tomorrow?

Lord, with You, I care for my **body** today . . .

Here is my food plan:

B

S

L

S

D

I remembered my water!

| 8 oz | 8 oz | 8 oz | 8 oz | 8 oz | 8 oz | 8 oz | 8 oz |

Alterations:

My plan for activity and rest:

Alterations:

Not every meal has to be perfect. While sticking with our food plan is important, at times we will need to adjust. This is just another sign of surrender.

Additional thoughts, notes, insight, goals, dreams . . .

DAY 42

Lord, with You, I care for my **spirit** today . . .

Fear not, for you will not be put to shame; and do not feel humiliated, for you will not be disgraced; but you will forget the shame of your youth . . . —ISAIAH 54:4 NASB

How have I allowed past shame and humiliation to hinder my current endeavors and my prosperous future?

Lord, with You, I care for my **emotions** today . . .

Emotions Check-In:

Lord, with You, I care for my **mind** today . . .

I will remember God's Word that His people will not be disgraced. I can release the shame of my youth.

What did I do well today (name at least one thing)?

What am I grateful for today?

What will I need God to help me with tomorrow?

Lord, with You, I care for my **body** today . . .

Here is my food plan:

B

S

L

S

D

I remembered my water!

Alterations:

My plan for activity and rest:

Alterations:

Replace one hour of late-night television with getting up one hour earlier in the morning for life-giving exercise.

Additional thoughts, notes, insight, goals, dreams . . .

DAY 43

Lord, with You, I care for my **spirit** today . . .

It will be like a woman experiencing the pains of labor. When her child is born, her anguish gives place to joy because she has brought a new person into the world.
—JOHN 16:21 NLT

In the process of losing it for life, what pains of labor must I experience in order to find joy?

Lord, with You, I care for my **emotions** today . . .

Emotions Check-In:

Lord, with You, I care for my **mind** today . . .

I will remember that I am bringing a new person into this world!

What did I do well today (name at least one thing)?

What am I grateful for today?

What will I need God to help me with tomorrow?

Lord, with You, I care for my **body** today . . .

Here is my food plan:

B

S

L

S

D

I remembered my water! [8 OZ] [8 OZ] [8 OZ] [8 OZ] [8 OZ] [8 OZ] [8 OZ] [8 OZ]

Alterations:

My plan for activity and rest:

Alterations:

Additional thoughts, notes, insight, goals, dreams . . .

DAY 44

Lord, with You, I care for my **spirit** today . . .

Just say a simple, "Yes, I will," or "No, I won't." Your word is enough. To strengthen your promise with a vow shows that something is wrong. —MATTHEW 5:37 NLT

How have I sabotaged my progress by making impossible goals and vows that I cannot keep?

Lord, with You, I care for my **emotions** today . . .

Emotions Check-In:

Lord, with You, I care for my **mind** today . . .

I will simply say "yes" to what's healthy and "no" to what's unhealthy.

What did I do well today (name at least one thing)?

What am I grateful for today?

What will I need God to help me with tomorrow?

Lord, with You, I care for my **body** today . . .

Here is my food plan:

B

S

L

S

D

I remembered my water!

Alterations:

My plan for activity and rest:

Alterations:

Though it may seem foreign to us for now, we will one day instinctively function in a healthier lifestyle. Practice makes progress!

Additional thoughts, notes, insight, goals, dreams . . .

DAY 45

Lord, with You, I care for my **spirit** today . . .

> . . . he is not far from each one of us. "For in him we live
> and move and have our being." —ACTS 17:27B-28

In what ways do I question God's involvement in my
weight-loss plan?

Lord, with You, I care for my **emotions** today . . .

Emotions Check-In:

Lord, with You, I care for my **mind** today . . .

> I will remain in the truth that You are not far from me;
> that You are present and sustain my very being.

What did I do well today (name at least one thing)?

What am I grateful for today?

What will I need God to help me with tomorrow?

Lord, with You, I care for my **body** today . . .

Here is my food plan:

B

S

L

S

D

I remembered my water!
Alterations:

My plan for activity and rest:

Alterations:

Additional thoughts, notes, insight, goals, dreams . . .

DAY 46

Lord, with You, I care for my **spirit** today . . .

> *Where there is no guidance the people fall, but*
> *in abundance of counselors there is victory.*
> —PROVERBS 11:14 NASB

Is it time to seek a professional counselor or spiritual
advisor to address the emotional scars that block my
recovery?

Lord, with You, I care for my **emotions** today . . .

Emotions Check-In:

Lord, with You, I care for my **mind** today . . .

> *I will open myself to support and guidance from others,*
> *including professionals, knowing that victory comes in*
> *the abundance of counsel.*

What did I do well today (name at least one thing)?

What am I grateful for today?

What will I need God to help me with tomorrow?

Lord, with You, I care for my **body** today . . .

Here is my food plan:

B

S

L

S

D

I remembered my water! 8 OZ 8 OZ 8 OZ 8 OZ 8 OZ 8 OZ 8 OZ 8 OZ

Alterations:

My plan for activity and rest:

Alterations:

Additional thoughts, notes, insight, goals, dreams . . .

DAY 47

Lord, with You, I care for my **spirit** today . . .

*So we fix our eyes not on what is seen, but on what is
unseen. For what is seen is temporary, but what is
unseen is eternal.* —2 CORINTHIANS 4:18

How can I turn my focus from food to God's will for
my eating habits today?

Lord, with You, I care for my **emotions** today . . .

Emotions Check-In:

Lord, with You, I care for my **mind** today . . .

*I will surrender my obsessions surrounding food and
cravings and focus on the eternal.*

What did I do well today (name at least one thing)?

What am I grateful for today?

What will I need God to help me with tomorrow?

Lord, with You, I care for my **body** today . . .

Here is my food plan:

B

S

L

S

D

I remembered my water!
Alterations:

| 8 OZ | 8 OZ | 8 OZ | 8 OZ | 8 OZ | 8 OZ | 8 OZ | 8 OZ |

My plan for activity and rest:

Alterations:

Additional thoughts, notes, insight, goals, dreams . . .

DAY 48

Lord, with You, I care for my **spirit** today . . .

*For our light and momentary troubles are achieving
for us an eternal glory that far outweighs them all.*
—2 CORINTHIANS 4:17

My problems with food and weight may seem tragic,
but they are light and momentary compared to what
God is achieving in me!

Lord, with You, I care for my **emotions** today . . .

Emotions Check-In:

Lord, with You, I care for my **mind** today . . .

*I will consider how my food and weight problems have
spiritual connections.*

What did I do well today (name at least one thing)?

What am I grateful for today?

What will I need God to help me with tomorrow?

Lord, with You, I care for my **body** today . . .

Here is my food plan:

B

S

L

S

D

I remembered my water! ⬜ ⬜ ⬜ ⬜ ⬜ ⬜ ⬜ ⬜

Alterations:

My plan for activity and rest:

Alterations:

Additional thoughts, notes, insight, goals, dreams . . .

DAY 49

Lord, with You, I care for my **spirit** today . . .

Why are you downcast, O my soul? Why so disturbed within me? — PSALM 42:5A

While dealing with food and weight issues, what angers me about this emotional journey of mine?

Lord, with You, I care for my **emotions** today . . .

Emotions Check-In:

Lord, with You, I care for my **mind** today . . .

I will pay attention and seek to understand what's bothering me so I don't feel the need to overeat.

What did I do well today (name at least one thing)?

What am I grateful for today?

What will I need God to help me with tomorrow?

Lord, with You, I care for my **body** today . . .

Here is my food plan:

B

S

L

S

D

I remembered my water! [8 OZ] [8 OZ] [8 OZ] [8 OZ] [8 OZ] [8 OZ] [8 OZ] [8 OZ]

Alterations:

My plan for activity and rest:

Alterations:

Additional thoughts, notes, insight, goals, dreams . . .

DAY 50

Lord, with You, I care for my **spirit** today . . .

An angry man stirs up dissension, and a hot-tempered one commits many sins. — PROVERBS 29:22

How have I dealt with anger toward my spouse, children, friends, boss, parents, or others? Toward myself?

Lord, with You, I care for my **emotions** today . . .

Emotions Check-In:

Lord, with You, I care for my **mind** today . . .

I realize that my anger can trigger out-of-control bingeing or excessive grazing.

What did I do well today (name at least one thing)?

What am I grateful for today?

What will I need God to help me with tomorrow?

Lord, with You, I care for my **body** today . . .

Here is my food plan:

B

S

L

S

D

I remembered my water! 🥤 🥤 🥤 🥤 🥤 🥤 🥤 🥤

Alterations:

My plan for activity and rest:

Alterations:

Additional thoughts, notes, insight, goals, dreams . . .

DAY 51

Lord, with You, I care for my **spirit** today . . .

My soul weeps because of grief; strengthen me
according to Your word. —PSALM 119:28 NASB

What am I learning about my grief on my spiritual
walk through the process of losing it for life?

Lord, with You, I care for my **emotions** today . . .

Emotions Check-In:

Lord, with You, I care for my **mind** today . . .

I will keep myself open and teachable, strengthened
according to Your Word.

What did I do well today (name at least one thing)?

What am I grateful for today?

What will I need God to help me with tomorrow?

Lord, with You, I care for my **body** today . . .

Here is my food plan:

B

S

L

S

D

I remembered my water!
Alterations:

| 8 oz | 8 oz | 8 oz | 8 oz | 8 oz | 8 oz | 8 oz | 8 oz |

My plan for activity and rest:

Alterations:

Additional thoughts, notes, insight, goals, dreams . . .

DAY 52

Lord, with You, I care for my **spirit** today . . .

A friend loves at all times, and a brother is born for adversity. — PROVERBS 17:17

What do I miss about my "old friend" food, and being able to eat whatever and whenever I wanted?

_____

_____

_____

Lord, with You, I care for my **emotions** today . . .

Emotions Check-In:

_____

_____

_____

Lord, with You, I care for my **mind** today . . .

I may be sad about losing my "friend," but I will remember that he has turned on me and robbed me of life. This friend does not love at all times.

What did I do well today (name at least one thing)?

_____

What am I grateful for today?

_____

What will I need God to help me with tomorrow?

_____

Lord, with You, I care for my **body** today . . .

Here is my food plan:

B

S

L

S

D

I remembered my water! 〔8 oz〕 〔8 oz〕 〔8 oz〕 〔8 oz〕 〔8 oz〕 〔8 oz〕 〔8 oz〕 〔8 oz〕

Alterations:

My plan for activity and rest:

Alterations:

Additional thoughts, notes, insight, goals, dreams . . .

DAY 53

Lord, with You, I care for my **spirit** today . . .

I cry aloud to the Lord; I lift up my voice to the Lord for mercy. I pour out my complaint before him; before him I tell my trouble. When my spirit grows faint within me, it is you who know my way. —PSALM 142:1-3A

What do I need from God on today's journey to recovery?

Lord, with You, I care for my **emotions** today . . .

Emotions Check-In:

Lord, with You, I care for my **mind** today . . .

When I am overwhelmed, God knows my path and what I need.

What did I do well today (name at least one thing)?

What am I grateful for today?

What will I need God to help me with tomorrow?

Lord, with You, I care for my **body** today . . .

Here is my food plan:

B

S

L

S

D

I remembered my water!

[8 OZ] [8 OZ] [8 OZ] [8 OZ] [8 OZ] [8 OZ] [8 OZ] [8 OZ]

Alterations:

My plan for activity and rest:

Alterations:

Build a list of non-food pleasures! Take a bubble bath, get a massage, read, bowl with friends, paint on a canvas, wash the car. These are all healthy and wonderful treats that can replace munching. They also serve as great rewards for progress.

Additional thoughts, notes, insight, goals, dreams . . .

DAY 54

Lord, with You, I care for my **spirit** today . . .

Therefore we do not lose heart. Though outwardly we are wasting away, yet inwardly we are being renewed day by day. —2 CORINTHIANS 4:16

In what ways is God renewing me so I do not lose heart today?

Lord, with You, I care for my **emotions** today . . .

Emotions Check-In:

Lord, with You, I care for my **mind** today . . .

I am grateful for the structure this program provides for my healing and renewal.

What did I do well today (name at least one thing)?

What am I grateful for today?

What will I need God to help me with tomorrow?

Lord, with You, I care for my **body** today . . .

Here is my food plan:

B

S

L

S

D

I remembered my water! [8 OZ] [8 OZ] [8 OZ] [8 OZ] [8 OZ] [8 OZ] [8 OZ] [8 OZ]

Alterations:

My plan for activity and rest:

Alterations:

Additional thoughts, notes, insight, goals, dreams . . .

DAY 55

Lord, with You, I care for my **spirit** today . . .

Be devoted to one another in brotherly love. . . . Share with
God's people who are in need. —ROMANS 12:10A, 13A

On this journey toward health and wholeness, what
do I need from others today? What can I give?

Lord, with You, I care for my **emotions** today . . .

Emotions Check-In:

Lord, with You, I care for my **mind** today . . .

For the long-term success of my recovery, I will
remember that I must give to and receive from others.

What did I do well today (name at least one thing)?

What am I grateful for today?

What will I need God to help me with tomorrow?

Lord, with You, I care for my **body** today . . .

Here is my food plan:

B

S

L

S

D

I remembered my water!

Alterations:

My plan for activity and rest:

Alterations:

Additional thoughts, notes, insight, goals, dreams . . .

DAY 56

Lord, with You, I care for my **spirit** today . . .

His mouth is sweetness itself; he is altogether lovely. This is my lover, this my friend . . . — SONG OF SONGS 5:16

How am I romancing my meals, snacks, and desserts?

Lord, with You, I care for my **emotions** today . . .

Emotions Check-In:

Lord, with You, I care for my **mind** today . . .

I will remember that food was never meant to fill the role of "lover" in my life.

What did I do well today (name at least one thing)?

What am I grateful for today?

What will I need God to help me with tomorrow?

Lord, with You, I care for my **body** today . . .

Here is my food plan:

B

S

L

S

D

I remembered my water!   8 OZ 8 OZ 8 OZ 8 OZ 8 OZ 8 OZ 8 OZ 8 OZ

Alterations:

My plan for activity and rest:

Alterations:

Additional thoughts, notes, insight, goals, dreams . . .

DAY 57

Lord, with You, I care for my **spirit** today . . .

The body is a unit, though it is made up of many parts; and though all its parts are many, they form one body. . . . If one part suffers, every part suffers with it; if one part is honored, every part rejoices with it. —1 CORINTHIANS 12:12A, 26

How have I deprived myself on diets and of the support God intends for my life "in the body"?

Lord, with You, I care for my **emotions** today . . .

Emotions Check-In:

Lord, with You, I care for my **mind** today . . .

In the past, I've tried alone and failed. Now, in fellowship with the body, I know that I have the support I need for success.

What did I do well today (name at least one thing)?

What am I grateful for today?

What will I need God to help me with tomorrow?

Lord, with You, I care for my **body** today . . .

Here is my food plan:

B

S

L

S

D

I remembered my water! 8 oz 8 oz 8 oz 8 oz 8 oz 8 oz 8 oz 8 oz

Alterations:

My plan for activity and rest:

Alterations:

Additional thoughts, notes, insight, goals, dreams . . .

DAY 58

Lord, with You, I care for my **spirit** today . . .

Therefore confess your sins to each other and pray for each other so that you may be healed. —*JAMES 5:16*

Am I willing to be honest with a friend and open myself to healing?

....

....

....

....

Lord, with You, I care for my **emotions** today . . .

Emotions Check-In:

....

....

....

....

Lord, with You, I care for my **mind** today . . .

I will trust that honest confession brings healing.

What did I do well today (name at least one thing)?

....

....

What am I grateful for today?

....

....

What will I need God to help me with tomorrow?

....

....

Lord, with You, I care for my **body** today . . .

Here is my food plan:

B

S

L

S

D

I remembered my water! 🥤 🥤 🥤 🥤 🥤 🥤 🥤 🥤

Alterations:

My plan for activity and rest:

Alterations:

TOP 10 CALORIE SOURCES TO AVOID (high in sugar, sodium, and fat):

White bread and rolls (white flour products)

Doughnuts, cookies, and cakes

Alcoholic beverages (very high in sugar)

Whole milk

Hamburgers, cheeseburgers, etc.

Beefsteaks, roasts

Soft drinks

Hot dogs, ham, lunchmeat (very high in sodium)

Eggs

Fries, chips

Additional thoughts, notes, insight, goals, dreams . . .

DAY 59

Lord, with You, I care for my **spirit** today . . .

Therefore, dear friends, since you already know this, be on your guard so that you may not be carried away by the error of lawless men and fall from your secure position. But grow in the grace and knowledge of our Lord and Savior Jesus Christ. To him be glory both now and forever! Amen. —2 PETER 3:17-18

How am I now on guard, setting boundaries around food and relationships, to protect my progress in losing it for life?

Lord, with You, I care for my **emotions** today . . .

Emotions Check-In:

Lord, with You, I care for my **mind** today . . .

I know that boundaries regarding food and others enable me to stay secure in recovery and continue to grow in grace.

What did I do well today (name at least one thing)?

What am I grateful for today?

What will I need God to help me with tomorrow?

Lord, with You, I care for my **body** today . . .

Here is my food plan:

B

S

L

S

D

I remembered my water! ⬛⬛⬛⬛⬛⬛⬛⬛
Alterations:

My plan for activity and rest:

Alterations:

Additional thoughts, notes, insight, goals, dreams . . .

DAY 60

Lord, with You, I care for my **spirit** today ...

> *Blessed is the man who perseveres under trial, because when he has stood the test, he will receive the crown of life that God has promised to those who love him.*
> —*JAMES 1:12*

In what ways have I persevered and "stood the test" in order to move toward my crown of life today?

Lord, with You, I care for my **emotions** today ...

Emotions Check-In:

Lord, with You, I care for my **mind** today ...

> *Rather than demanding instant results from fad diets, I will persist in my daily routine of surrender.*

What did I do well today (name at least one thing)?

What am I grateful for today?

What will I need God to help me with tomorrow?

Lord, with You, I care for my **body** today ...

Here is my food plan:

B

S

L

S

D

I remembered my water!

[8 OZ] [8 OZ] [8 OZ] [8 OZ] [8 OZ] [8 OZ] [8 OZ] [8 OZ]

Alterations:

My plan for activity and rest:

Alterations:

The problem may be physical; the cause may be emotional; the solution is surely spiritual.

Additional thoughts, notes, insight, goals, dreams ...

APPENDIX A

Before I nibble in excess . . .

· What triggered my craving?

· If I choose to eat this, what effect will it have on me?

· If I lay down this treat, what challenge/feeling do I face?

· What is a healthier way I could deal with this situation?

If I stray from my plan . . .

· Stop the eating behavior, and ask God for help.

· Make a phone call for support.

· Record what I've eaten.

I will not beat myself up! I will . . .

· Forgive myself.

· Pray for willingness to continue with normal meal plans.

· Realize that one slip does not mean the end of my program.

· Remind myself: I can start afresh right now!

Great is his faithfulness; his mercies begin afresh each day.

—*LAMENTATIONS 3:23 NLT*

THE TOTAL SOLUTION
—PHYSICAL, EMOTIONAL, SPIRITUAL—
FOR PERMANENT WEIGHT LOSS

LOSE IT *for* LIFE

STEPHEN ARTERBURN & DR. LINDA MINTLE

No diet, pill or surgery can give you God's tools to Lose It For Life.

But this book can.

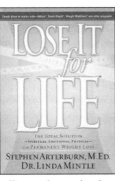

Most diet programs only tell you what to eat or how to exercise. And when you're done with them, the pounds return. *Lose It For Life* is a uniquely balanced, total solution that focuses on your mind, body and soul—and how the emotional, mental and spiritual factors affect your weight. Ultimately, this solution—developed by best-selling author and radio personality Stephen Arterburn, who lost 60 pounds 20 years ago and has kept it off—helps readers achieve what they desire most: permanent results.

Using the principles from the nationally recognized Lose It For Life Seminars, this groundbreaking book is the perfect companion to any weight-loss program—Atkins, South Beach, Weight Watchers, whatever! And it's co-authored by Dr. Linda Mintle, whose clinical work in eating disorders gives even more hope to those who have tried diet fads with disappointing results.

This book will give you the information and motivation you need to live a healthy life and to finally *Lose It For Life!*

ISBN: 1-59145-245-7
PRICE: $22.99 U.S.

Lose It For Life for Teens
Steve Arterburn & Ginger Garrett

Weight is such a critical issue with teenagers. They are overwhelmed with messages that present unrealistic and unhealthy body images. *Lose It For Life for Teens* will save them a lifetime of struggles and negative self-perceptions. It will help young people:

- set the right goals
- deal with emotional triggers for overeating
- understand how to lose weight in a healthy way and keep it off
- design a customized work-out program
- realize the power, comfort and relational support God offers.

ISBN: 1-59145-248-1   PRICE: $12.99

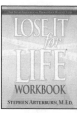

Lose It For Life Workbook

This companion workbook helps participants to better apply the program to their specific situation. It is also ideal for group study, helping facilitate meetings for those who want to encourage each other in their journey toward better physical and spiritual health.

ISBN: 1-59145-275-9   PRICE: $13.99 U.S.

Lose It For Life Day by Day Devotional

God is interested in all of our problems, but surprisingly, many Christians neglect or are reluctant to bring their struggles with weight issues to Him. *The Lose It For Life Day by Day Devotional* will help Lose It For Lifers draw daily spiritual encouragement from the One who loves us most and is interested in every aspect of our lives—even our struggles with weight.

ISBN: 1-59145-249-X   PRICE: $13.99 U.S.

Lose It For Life Journal Planner

The *Lose It For Life Journal Planner* is a vital tool that will help participants plan for success and record results on their journey toward optimum health. It also includes valuable specific support for those days when temptation is hitting hardest.

ISBN: 1-59145-274-0   PRICE: $9.99 U.S.

Lose It For Life® INSTITUTE

Your life doesn't have to be defined by what you weigh.

For more information on upcoming events call **1.800.NEW.LIFE**